ENDORSEMENTS

"Pam has penned a powerful word that will encourage many who have been waiting for their long-awaited promises to manifest; those who have gone through many dark nights of the soul and are still wondering, "When, Lord?" Her life story is a perfect example of how the Lord captures our tears and through them, releases a mighty anointing in us to minister to others. Through her own stream of tears, she allowed the Lord to instruct and fashion her so that what she now has to give is pure and enduring hope to others. Her love for the Word and for science blend together to reveal heavenly wisdom that activates awe and wonder in the places where we have felt despair and hopelessness. I believe that after reading this book, a new level of faith will arise in your heart and like me, you'll want to pass this book along to others that need revival in their heart, too!"

Laura K. Judah

Champion Builders Center

"It is my great honor, delight, and pleasure to recommend this work of art Yahweh has given my precious friend, Pamela Holecheck to steward. As I read this I realized how transformative this work will be for anyone reading it. Pam lights the path back to wholeness in such a beautiful and powerful way; giving tools for the mind, soul, and body during times of great loss, trauma, and deep trials. As I read, "Vial Of Liquid Pearl," I became aware that this treasure will be used to take the teeth out of the lies that difficulty, loss, and trauma define us. This treasure restores the reader back to Truth, that we live in and from HOPE and LOVE."

Kymberly Whitman

Heart of the Bride Ministries

"Pam, we love and admire you. You are a testimony and inspiration to many, both here and abroad. Thank you for sharing your journey so transparently with us. May others discover their solutions in Christ through reading your book."

Eddie Smith

Executive Director, U.S. Prayer Center

ACKNOWLEDGMENTS

Grateful to:

Tanya Dorris for sharing the vision you had during prayer. Here is the fruit of that.

The many who have supported me with friendship, encouragement, prayer, financially, with hospitality, and countless other ways, without whom I wouldn't have a story to tell.

Eddie, for your input and direction. This book won't be going to Heaven with me!

Laura, Tanya, Kym, Gabi, Gary, and Lisa among others for your help, input and inspiration with this first-time book process.

My family for your love and support as I lived and traveled the globe.

My spiritual family near and far who have been an important part of my life's story. Your prayers and encouragement through this process are woven into this story and others to come.

Most importantly to my Heavenly Father, Yeshua, and Holy Spirit without whom none of this would be. May you all be glorified in a way that brings Your Kingdom to Earth in increased measures.

DEDICATION

I dedicate this book to my amazing Mom who read countless books to me as a child. Our mutual love of reading led to my love of writing. Her grace and dignity maintained throughout years of health issues, leaves me in awe and wonder that I was so privileged to be her daughter.

I love and miss you, Mom. This tear is for you.

CONTENTS

INTRODUCTION

This book began during a dark season of many tears and a prophetic word given by my friend, Tanya. Since then I have been able to share it with those who grieve. However, tears come from many sources which include joy, onions, hope, fear, etc. So we will take a look at the various forms.

I love science and the Bible, and when combined, it is impressive to see how our Father in His wisdom has hidden clues for us to discover. Proverbs 25:2 tells us it is His glory to conceal things, but our glory is to search them out. As we do so, we gain ownership of the discovery for us to steward.

As you will read, each tear shed carries a unique message within its DNA.

I desire that all who read this will receive comfort, hope, and understanding of the beauty in each one of their tears. Please share it with those who need encouragement or a better understanding of the importance of their tears, for they are a gift from our Creator, with each one telling a story. May we embrace them as such to be utilized and celebrated!

Feel free to use this for meditation, a guide into the Courts of Heaven, or to give to someone in need of comfort and freedom regarding tears. It is not a typical look at grief or sympathy, but a unique glimpse into the story behind each tear.

The Hebrew Names of God the Father have been chosen. I prefer YHWH, Yahweh, or Creator. I have also taken the liberty of using the Hebrew name of Jesus our Messiah, Yeshua. My choice in doing so is one of honoring their original names since they have changed throughout history.

I discovered the work of Hans Jenny[1], a Swiss Scientist who used a tonoscope to make sound visible on things such as sand and water. He discovered that the frequencies of the vowels spoken from the Hebrew alphabet impacted the sand in a way that it took on the shape of the written symbols when spoken; whereas modern languages did not generate the same results.

Our bodies are made up of an average of 60-80% water. Water amplifies sound. Therefore, I desire that we make the most impact with our words. The letter "J" is not in the original 1611 King James version of the Bible. Instead, it was written "Iesus." Originally, the name of Messiah was יֲשׁוע, pronounced Yahushua or Yeshua.

He intends to restore His name according to Zechariah 14:9, "Then YHVH shall be king over all the earth, in that day shall there be one LORD, and his name one

CHAPTER ONE

Tears in a Vial

As my friend Tanya prayed for me during a difficult season in my life, she saw the Lord holding a vial with liquid pearl in it. Though I found it interesting, I wasn't sure what it meant for me. Shortly after this happened, I read an article on the study of tears under a microscope. I then realized Yahweh was saying that this vial of liquid pearl represented my tears that He was holding for me.

Psalm 56:8 (AMP, NLT)

You number and record my wanderings; put my tears into Your bottle—are they not in Your book? You keep track of all my sorrows, You have collected all my tears in your bottle, You have recorded each one in your book.

Psalm 38:9 (TPT)

Lord, you know all my desires and deepest longings.
My tears are liquid words, and you can read them all.

Psalm 39:12 (TPT)

Lord, listen to all my tender cries. Read my every tear,
like liquid words that plead for your help. I feel all alone
at times, like a stranger to you, passing through this life
just like all those before me.

The word bottle also means vial[2] in Hebrew. It is referring here
to the fact that our tears are kept and recorded.

In ancient Judea, mourners would leave a glass vial filled with
their tears in the tomb of their loved one after they died. These vials
contained iridescent colors, similar to liquid pearl that Tanya had seen.
How beautiful of the Lord to be holding this vial of my tears.

Rose-Lynn Fisher decided to look at her tears to see if they
would look different with her various forms of emotions. She studied
100 different tears and found that basal tears, the ones that our body
produces to lubricate our eyes, are drastically different from the tears that
happen while we are chopping onions. The tears from hard laughter are
entirely different to those of sorrow. Like a drop of ocean water, each
tiny teardrop carries a microcosm of human experience.

Her project is called, "The Topography of Tears"[3]. The whole article about her journey is quite fascinating. Please take a look at the tears. Some of those tears included:

Tears of change.

Tears of grief.

Tears of joy.

Tears from onions.

Tears of redemption.

Tears of timeless reunion.

Tears of remembrance.

Tears of possibility and hope.

They are all uniquely different from one another.

According to Joseph Stromberg[4] of the Smithsonian's College of Arts, there are three major types of tears: basal, reflex, and psychic—which are triggered by emotions. All tears contain substances such as oils, antibodies, and enzymes suspended in salt water. Each tear has distinct molecules making them unique. Emotional tears have painkilling hormones which are released when we are stressed. Plus, the tears seen under the microscope are crystallized salt and can lead to different shapes and forms. So even psychic tears with the same chemical composition can look very different.

Like snowflakes, fingerprints, and DNA, no tears are alike. The difference between all of these is fascinating.

The Japanese scientist Dr. Masaru Emoto[5] studied water crystals and sound, along with the effects of spoken and written words. Their responses were either negative or positive depending if what they were experiencing was positive or negative.

Quantum Theory suggests that all matter has memory as well as frequencies and energy. Water amplifies sound, and our bodies are made up of around 60-80% water, and our brains 90% water. Therefore, what we think, say, and listen to can either increase or decrease the frequencies in our bodies. Science shows that disease and parasites cannot live in an environment where positive frequencies are higher. Both light and sound are frequencies. When our Creator spoke creation into existence, He used both. Since we are made in His image, what we think, speak, and listen to will significantly affect us since the water within us amplifies everything. Water and salt make up the chemistry of tears. Therefore, according to Rose-Lynn Fisher's photos, the water in tears seem to be able to communicate the emotions connected with them. So what we think, feel, and speak all have a powerful effect on us.

Tanya shared the picture she saw of the vial of tears with me during one of the darkest and most difficult seasons of my life. I had experienced tremendous loss and grief on many levels, and had shed so many tears that I marveled how any one person could produce so many. How comforting to know that He keeps each one, recorded, and deemed as precious in His sight. To me, that speaks of the value of each tear as well as the corresponding emotion. Nothing wasted, overlooked, or diminished in our lives where our Father is concerned.

Ever.

CHAPTER TWO

My Story

As this book was finishing, I was prompted to share my story to reveal how this book and theme came about, and why tears were an essential part of it. I am vague in some places to protect others.

From an early age, I learned how not to show emotion, especially sadness or tears which then built up layers of vows including,

"I will not cry!"

"I will not show any emotion, especially weakness, it isn't safe to let them know that they are getting to me."

"People who cry are weak—I can't believe that they can't control themselves," etc.

Marrying at 18 meant growing up quickly as I experienced a lifetime within a few short years, including a miscarriage. Since I didn't know that I was pregnant until it happened, there was no grieving as I hadn't bonded with the baby or the idea of being pregnant. Years later while reading, "Tilly" by Frank Perretti about aborted babies being cared for by Yeshua in Heaven, the deep crying began. I read this shortly after my Grandmother whom I was close to passed away. I knew enough by this time about inner healing to recognize that this level of crying was more than just about the book I was reading.

Yahweh revealed that I was grieving my child, a girl, and to name her. So I did after both of my Grandmothers— Christina Rose. He let me know that my Grandmother was telling her all about me, and this was the first time that I had grieved over the loss of my child— eleven years after the miscarriage.

A few years later another time of grieving came when she would have been 16. I wrote her a letter in my journal which assisted the process even further. It was a beautiful time of healing, and the tears that came were from a deep place within. Since then, there have been a few times of grieving her. As my mother was passing, I was able to speak to her about her granddaughter so that she could tell her even more about our family and me. I think of her around the time of year that I miscarried, and again when she would have been born. I have spiritual daughters who are around the same age, so Father has blessed me in return. Mother's Day is still a bit hard, but the grieving is soft and brief.

The next event which nearly destroyed me was when I discovered that my husband and close friend/co-worker had betrayed me. My world came crashing in on me. I couldn't breathe. There was nowhere to go, which is when the next set of beliefs and vows erected:

"I can't trust anyone"
"never open your heart up to anyone that way again"
"I wouldn't do that to anyone, how could they do that to me?" etc.

Divorce was not as common then as it is now, so on top of feeling betrayed with nearly unbearable pain, was the shame of it. I was then asked to return a family heirloom.

I decided to start life over and moved to Houston, TX. Shortly after my 25th birthday, I bought a house due to making so much money as a hairstylist, that I needed a tax break since Houston was known as, "Boom Town." However, only a few months later it was known as, "Bust Town." The oil industry took a nose dive and with it most of my clientele. Since I worked on commission, I was in dire straits which led me to surrender my life to the Lord.

I ended up losing my house a couple of years later anyway. That was another loss which the Lord used to work deep healing in my soul. It was during this time that I met some of my life-long friends that opened up the pathway to where I am today.

One of them introduced me into missions, and after my first mission trips with her I eventually gave up my career as a hairstylist to move overseas.

It takes years to build up a clientele, so it was not an easy decision to switch careers. I sold almost everything, gave up my apartment, sold my car, even gave my dog to my previous roommate. Shortly after— even after numerous confirmations along the way that our team was a "go" for moving overseas, it was shut down! We were all devastated! Now I was without a job/career, home and most furnishings, car, and dog.

Around this time another group of new friends became my spiritual family. There was a deep level of fellowship that enriched my life. Father used this group to love on me in a needed way. For several years when asked how I was doing, I would burst into tears. I tried so hard not to and would tell myself beforehand that I wasn't going to cry, but when asked how I was doing— tears! They started handing me the tissue box as I walked in…so much for dignity.

The journey of inner healing had begun and the vows to never cry uncovered and removed. Where tears had been locked up for years, they now flowed freely and abundantly as I was starting life over once again.

After working in a law firm for a couple of years while living with my spiritual parents, the time came to go into full-time ministry. Being immersed in Youth With A Mission brought even more profound healing; the 24/7 atmosphere served as an incubator for further healing as we learned how to be discipled to disciple others. The following stood out to me during this time:

2 Corinthians 1:3-7 (AMP)

3 Blessed [gratefully praised and adored] be the God and Father of our Lord Jesus Christ, the Father of mercies and the God of all comfort, 4 who comforts and encourages us in every trouble so that we will be able to comfort and encourage those who are in any kind of trouble, with the comfort with which we ourselves are comforted by God. 5 For just as Christ's sufferings are ours in abundance [as they overflow to His followers], so also our comfort [our reassurance, our encouragement, our consolation] is abundant through Christ [it is truly more than enough to endure what we must]. 6 But if we are troubled and distressed, it is for your comfort and salvation; or if we are comforted and encouraged, it is for your comfort, which works [in you] when you patiently endure the same sufferings which we experience. 7 And our hope for you [our confident expectation of good for you] is firmly grounded [assured and unshaken], since we know that just as you share as partners in our sufferings, so also you share as partners in our comfort.

The ministry of comfort began here. Father was redeeming my pain and loss, so I could extend compassion to others as they came for counsel, prayer, and ministry.

Being in ministry was not the end of loss, grief, or challenging circumstances. It was quite the opposite! I was now a threat to the enemy, and the unredeemed areas of my life became his target. Though I did not have the understanding or language that I now do regarding the Courts of Heaven and adjudicating things from there, I knew there had to be a way to freedom here on earth since everything finished at the Cross.

I am a forerunner/pioneer, therefore, most often working with visionaries and projects from the beginning. It's usually messy, but those messes have become opportunities for more growth from the place of desperation.

One such difficulty happened after moving to another state. It required each of us getting apartments instead of living in a community as I had for years. Friends blessed me with a shower of sorts, giving me new things to furnish my first apartment in 10 years with, so I was excited! However, shortly after making this transition and settling in, we were told of significant changes to the original vision. The short of it is—another ministry disaster! We scattered with most of us feeling the breath knocked out of us. Though it never resolved in what I would consider a healthy way, we each had to walk it out with the Lord. Over the years many of us have reconnected in various ways, but not in the same way.

After this experience, I was left unsure about doing ministry, and contemplated another career change. While visiting a friend in Germany, I had an encounter where my body began to shake, and a voice spoke so clearly inside that it seemed audible! It said, "You WILL be living here!" Father knew this was the only way I would make such a move.

Nine years after moving to Germany, my Mom became terminally ill. Though she had been sick most of her life, this was different. It meant frequent extended trips which eventually took a toll on my finances, ministry in Germany, and my health. I couldn't be 100% in either place, which led to the difficult decision to move back to America. It was a long and challenging process as things are more complicated in Germany.

Months before the move back while returning to Germany from a ministry trip, I had a layover in Cairo, Egypt where I was delayed for days and along with many others, had to be evacuated during what is now referred to as, "The Arab Spring." With all that I was facing with Mom, ministry, and possibly moving back, this incident confirmed that I should go to a debriefing ministry for a week, which I did.

There I learned valuable tools, including that trauma survivors need time and a safe place to tell their story uninterrupted. Together with another gal working with an NGO (Non-government organization), that deals with disasters; we took turns sharing our stories. The guidelines were that while the other was telling their story, we were to sit and listen without making any noise—not even a "hmmm," no nodding of the head, nothing! We could only ask a question if we didn't understand something. A significant part of healing comes through telling the story. That was a learning experience which would assist me in the life changes that were about to take place as well as reshape my ministry.

I sold a few things and gave most away. My beautiful apartment was a significant part of my ministry, and the decor released peace and a sense of "home." My guest room was always open for fellow ministry friends to stay, while others loved to come and "be." I sent a huge box and a couple of large suitcases with my most treasured possessions back to America. The box containing things like years worth of journals, books, photos, favorite movies on DVD's, and CD's, cost nearly $100 to send.

It never arrived.

Heartbreak

Shortly after the move, I got into a relationship for the first time in 30 years. To fully appreciate the range of emotions that came forth during this time, I will give a brief history.

After my divorce, I had a relationship that ended after a year with him cheating on me. This now established pattern would take years before I knew how to deal with it. Shortly after this breakup, I gave my life to the Lord. In my naiveté, I believed I would now meet spiritually and emotionally healthy men I could trust and we would live happily ever after. It was my Christian Fairytale.

My first experience was in an adult singles group where I struck up a friendship with a guy around my age. He began calling me, and we would spend hours on the phone. Previous experiences outside of the church would have meant that he was interested and the beginning of something. One night while attending a church single's event, I discovered he was absent due to picking up his fiancé at the airport! Interesting how that never came up during the many long late night conversations.

Over the years since then, I had other similar friendships develop that kept me waiting for something more to happen. After wondering what their intentions were and getting tired of waiting, I would eventually ask them. The responses were mostly, "just friends," or, "you're like a sister." I want to interject here that I have two brothers who have never looked at or treated me like that. My heart was broken over and over as it seemed their emotional and spiritual needs were met without any commitment on their part.

As I traveled internationally and young women would discover my age and singleness, repeatedly I heard similar stories and would minister to their broken hearts. Often it seemed the Church was just as dysfunctional, if not more so, than in the world. At least in the world, I knew what their intentions were and could decide from there.

With my background and very brief history, I wanted to share a glimpse into the heartbreak and disappointment I experienced with men, causing many tears to shed. The confusion, feeling used, and most of all, rejection over and over again was made worse since I had expected something better from Christian men.

I had been in another such situation with a guy before moving back to America where it seemed there was interest beyond friendship, but I remained guarded due to my past experiences. After inquiring and receiving no answer, I moved on. Around this time a friend asked if she could set me up, and I agreed to it.

At first, I was scared and tried to set him up with another friend of mine, but he only wanted to get to know me. How refreshing, especially now that I had just moved back to America with a fresh start in life.

I had not realized until this relationship how starved my soul was and my heart guarded. Due to our long-distance relationship, we had the opportunity to discover one another through emails, texts, and phone calls. I didn't see a photo of him for the first couple of months so I could get to know him on another level. This relationship was one of the few bright spots in my life as it gave me something to look forward to each day while Mom was fading away.

There was finally romance in my life—friends and family were breathing a sigh of relief! It blessed Mom to see me so happy. Gift-giving being his love language meant that I was showered with gifts. This missionary who had lived on a limited income for years was now overwhelmed with delight. He listened to me, and always had encouraging words for me that brightened those dark days.

After a couple of months, while communicating with the other guy who had not answered me about his feelings, I let him know about my new relationship. He then shared about his feelings for me. After 30 years of no one, now there were two. Really? The situation was another emotional roller coaster, but after conversations, thought and prayer, I decided to further explore the relationship I was in since the other guy wasn't able to commit at that time. I felt this would work best for both of us, and thankfully we have remained friends.

A few months later as the relationship was settling in more, I discovered things that concerned me and broke up with him. We kept in touch which made the gradual process of letting go easier since it was during the end stages of Mom's life. Since he lives in Texas, I thought we could work on the relationship after I returned.

I was privileged to be with my Mom when she passed. Since she'd been sick for years, the moment I saw that she had transitioned, tears of relief and joy came knowing she was no longer suffering. However, the grieving tears did come. A week later there was a divorce in the family. As a friend stated—I was experiencing all of the significant stressors at once, and it was having a negative impact on my health.

While driving back to Texas, the man I had broken up with and was hoping to reconcile with called as he knew I was returning. He informed me that he was seeing someone else. In retrospect, I had suspected something, but he kindly waited to let me know until after Mom passed.

For the first time since moving back to America, I had to figure out what to do with my life, and all I saw was a big black hole. There was nothing that I could see before me. With this news, my life imploded! Though I was returning to Texas, I had no home, no ministry, no money. I had just lost my Mom, and the only thing I had to look forward to, was the possibility of reconciling with him. He owns a business and lives in a beautiful house in a great area. That indeed would have covered many areas of concern, but I just couldn't compromise.

I spent two days in a hotel in Hot Springs, AR. never leaving the room. I ordered room service and cried non-stop day and night. I was shattered with unbearable pain.

There's something about romantic emotions that seems to go deeper than any other, at least that has been my experience.

I can see now that all of these events worked like a surgical knife opening up the deep wounds all at once, and I was hemorrhaging.

On the morning of 12-21-12, the day many believed would be the end of the world, I woke up early and sat on the balcony watching the sunrise. I wrote in my journal words from the Lord about this being a new dawn and beginning for me. I then heard,

Isaiah 43:18-19 (NKJV)

"Do not remember the former things, Nor consider the things of old.19
Behold, I will do a new thing, Now it shall spring forth;
Shall you not know it? I will even make a road in the wilderness
And rivers in the desert."

Those words gave me the strength to pack up my car and drive to Texas unaware of all that I was about to face. As I left the hotel, I decided on a different route, and as I left the city, there was a sign which read, "Highway of Hope." I later drove through Hope, AR. and shortly after contacted a friend in Houston who agreed to let me hide out at her place for a while. In her guest room was a plaque with one word, HOPE. She had named it, "The Hope Room," and that was my re-entry.

Back in Texas

After hiding out at my friend's and allowing the shock of everything to settle a bit, I felt pressure to let people know where I was geographically and emotionally. I made the wrong assumption that since the majority of people had known me for about 20 years, that they would understand I was not myself—and I wasn't. I was in shock. I later learned that I was experiencing PTSD.

I was aware of the love and concern of many for me during this time and how they wanted the best for me. However, I learned a painful lesson on how not to treat a person in this situation. As each well-meaning person gave their input and advice, I would shrink more and more into isolation.

I shared my debriefing experience hoping to be allowed to tell my story. I discovered that I was usually the one listening due to my background of being a hairstylist and counselor which often was a one-way conversation. When I began to shift the narrative, it caused the boat to rock. Now that I needed to talk and be heard, it was difficult to find. I recognized some of it was due to wanting to help me, but it had the opposite effect. I saw how uncomfortable the others would be towards listening for various reasons. We have many great qualities but listening—truly listening, is not one of them.

A friend shared from her disaster relief training an acronym they use for this very reason:

WAIT: **W**hy **A**m **I** **T**alking? I like that!

The best analogy of how I was feeling, was that of a person with 3rd-degree burns in intensive care. They are in unbearable pain, with limited visitors due to the risk of infection and death. The slightest thing causes excruciating pain. It takes a long time for each layer to heal while the scar tissue forms. That was my soul! I was so raw and vulnerable that things which to most might seem like nothing, caused excruciating pain. Therefore, I felt the need to establish boundaries in written form since that was all the energy I had to offer.

The email I had sent was not well accepted or understood by some as I wrongly assumed it would be. However, I did receive a lot of positive feedback from fellow missionaries and those in ministry who thanked me for putting into words what they were unable to, and how much it helped them. So it was a bittersweet moment of stepping out and not allowing fear to dumb me down anymore. Sadly, I ended up paying a high price by losing most of my financial support and friendships suffered. More loss and unneeded stress. Would this hellish nightmare ever end?

Around this time my Doctor diagnosed me with adrenal exhaustion along with menopause. I could barely function feeling the pressure to show up with a smile and doing well.

Suddenly the book of Job had become more real to me than ever before. His friends did well in the beginning as they sat quietly mourning with him. Their "good advice" is what got them into trouble with The Most High, as He corrected them for it. Perhaps there is a lesson here for all of us.

Now came the long process of going through the stages of grief, which included much ugly crying.

Where to begin?

With Mom's death?

My move back to America I had hoped never to do?

The relationship(s) issues?

The loss of my life in Germany, friends, ministry, the box of precious things?

How to deal with the confusion over my identity? I'm now neither American nor German but a mix.

How and where do I fit?

Longtime friendships that were not the same?

The loss of financial support because I was no longer living overseas or able to perform as expected?

My health?

I entered the anger stage of grief. Feeling as though I was not being heard or understood caused me to feel even more alone, isolated, and angry. Attending any event did not feel safe. Sunday mornings were so stressful in planning how to arrive late, then leave early enough to avoid the most dreaded of all questions—"How are you?" Finally, I stopped going. The very places where I should have felt safe didn't provide the safety or comfort that I needed.

Other dear friends came with their well-meaning advice which only compounded my pain. I kept a mental note and wrote down what it felt like to feel so vulnerable and broken and not have anyone listen or know how to help. That process will be explained further in another book that I started during this season so I could clearly remember how it felt.

I sought help and found a ministry trained to listen. I shared my story, and the facilitators asked questions to help me get to the subconscious beliefs where the pain was buried. It saved my life.

Thankfully, I had friends who did listen and loved on me. When thanked, they said they often didn't know what to say or do to help me, but for me that was okay. I've come to realize that some people need to understand that it is okay not to have the answers but to merely listen. When someone is in deep pain, they need an outlet and safe place to "be" and tell their story if and when they are ready. "Exhale" was the word that best described what was needed. I am so thankful to those dear friends who allowed that.

I had choices to make during this time. Would I keep going or give up? I was tempted to quit. Hours, days, weeks, months, and even years were spent forgiving, releasing, letting go, blessing those who had wounded me, and on and on. It was all part of the healing journey. Sure, in some cases I had the right to be upset, but to hang on to it would have cost much, much more, and it just wasn't worth it. I entered into the fellowship of His suffering that Paul referred to in Philippians 3:10.

I was lamenting to the Lord one day about how alone and misunderstood I felt. He lovingly said, "I know how you feel." It wasn't in a diminishing way, but as He spoke to my heart I was suddenly transported to the Garden of Gethsemane where His closest friends were asleep when He needed them most. At that moment, I knew that He knew everything I was experiencing and feeling as He had felt it all Himself. The tears flowed as I melted into Him experiencing this precious moment together. Finally, someone got it. I realized all I needed was for someone to understand and acknowledge my pain. He was the only one who ever fully could, and I am so thankful for that life-changing moment of revelation!

After a couple of years in Houston, I moved to the Austin area. Not far from where I lived was a road called, "New Hope." The hope theme continued through the healing and ongoing equipping process that has brought me to this point of my journey. My friend Kym Whitman mentored me in the Courts of Heaven. It was through this, the Theophostic Prayer (now known as Transformation Prayer) that I had received in Houston, along with many other modalities I sought out of desperation, that have helped me so much. I am still in process but am much more whole.

Generational and bloodline issues which had caused trauma throughout my generations have been dealt with, which had opened me up to some of the things that had happened. Along with that, I took responsibility for my responses and reactions to those things. This has taken work, but to see the good fruit testifies of it working. Now Yeshua's blood answers for those things in the Courts of Heaven. I have divorce papers from things like trauma, betrayal, abuse, even divorce. What a response to years of crying out for freedom!

Recently a friend was going through a challenging time. She reached out to a few of us for prayer, and each of us did what we often do—gave Christian patronizing canned answers, Scriptures, advice, etc., including me. Holy Spirit gently reminded me of what that felt like, and I immediately wrote her and apologized for doing the very thing that I hated done to me during my difficult time. Since I was no longer feeling the way I had back then, how easy it was to slip into "fix-it" mode when all she needed was to know that someone understands and that she is loved.

She responded in tears that finally someone got it. She needed that safe place to tell her story uninterrupted, though she didn't even know how to verbalize it. I had forgotten. Even after all I had gone through, I still forgot. That was a gentle reminder to forgive and extend grace and mercy to those who are clueless—including me. I am not as triggered when someone responds to me with their well-meaning advice as those deep-seated beliefs, offenses, lies, hurts, and other things are healing. I asked Holy Spirit again never to let me forget how I felt during that season. I love and honor each friend and understand better now that they were hurting for me and desperately wanted to help the only way they knew how. I am grateful for the healing it worked in me, and I want to use what I learned to help others. That is the reason I share my story.

It's been seven years since I moved back to America and life has not been the same. I continue living with the effects and often question the decision since it has been the hardest season of my life. Yet, having that last year with Mom and being with her as she transitioned was the greatest blessing. This process has worked something deep within that has changed me forever. It has squeezed more tears out of me than I ever thought humanly possible...but each one recorded as you will read about in following chapters. I will reap joy!

I hope my story will help those who have much to grieve, as well as those who don't know how to allow others to do so. It's to share a glimpse into the need for tears, for grieving, and for letting yourself and others do so in a healthy way.

May we get this! There are many people with deep wounds, trauma, grief, and if we are to be the sources of healing and wholeness— we MUST get this. If that means we go through healing to deal with whatever it is that causes us to be unable to give someone else space to tell their story, to grieve and not make it about us, then let's do it. The world is in pain and in need of a safe place to tell their story and heal. May we mature and create safe places for others to "Exhale".

Can we allow Yahweh to bring us to those hidden places in us first for healing and freedom?

Let's allow the tears to come for He holds them in a vial.

CHAPTER THREE

Each Tear Is Precious

As I meditated on tears after Tanya's word to me, I saw how all of this works together. The Lord spoke to me regarding this vial of liquid pearl:

I hold each tear as a precious pearl.

The liquid pearl is your tears. The hurts, disappointments, irritations, as well as

the tears of joy, excitement, and relief! Each one is having their own bottle because

they are so very dear and precious to Me.

Each one carrying a story — your story.

Your journey.

Your prayers.

As you have sown in tears, you will reap joy! That is My promise to you!

Weeping has lasted for a very long night, but My joy is coming as it's dawning a

new day. Each tear has sown a seed that will reap an abundant harvest of joy.

These tears have softened hard ground in your personal life, as well as spiritually. As you continue to plow through hard places, these tears moisten the ground allowing you to go deeper and breakthrough — each one carrying a bit of My DNA as well as yours. I have wept with you. Our DNA has mingled. So you see, there can only be a good harvest that comes from this.

There is also a fragrance and vibration connected with each one. There is cleansing in your soul as well as your body. Your spirit mingled with Mine is also involved doing My will through them. Tears are an amazing gift from Me. Now take this revelation and run with it. I will give you more, and you will share it with others.

Tears are words the heart can't express. ——Author Unknown

Here is some creative space for you to process your own thoughts for what the Lord may be speaking to you about your own tears and journey with Him.

CHAPTER FOUR

Archive of Tears

Shortly after I received this word from the Lord, I was watching Sid Roth's, "It's Supernatural". His guest was Dennis Walker[6] who described a visit to Heaven where he saw archives of tears connected with prayer.

He saw a woman praying for her son and weeping for him. The Lord then spoke to him:

Every tear is remembered here. Every tear is kept. Every seed of the saint's suffering is kept in Heaven. This is the body of evidence that will be presented at the judgment of the fallen angels.

Every tear that is caused by their sowing the seed of rebellion will be brought to the trial and be shown here.

Those things will be kept for an eternity of the inheritors of salvation so the angels would know the reason as it's kept especially for them.

I find it amazing that the Lord so treasures each one of our tears, each kept as a reminder and memorial for eternity. I am again reminded of

Psalm 56:8 (NKJV) (NIV)

You number and record my wanderings; put my tears into Your bottle—are they not in Your book?
Record my misery; list my tears on your scroll are they not in your record?

What book or scroll? I discovered there are many books in Heaven. The Hebrew word for book is cepherרפס [7], which also means: letter, evidence, bill, register, scroll.

As an intercessor, I am no stranger to tears in the place of prayer. At times I am only able to weep and sense that each tear is carrying what I cannot put into words before the Throne of Grace. Tears are prayers, too. They travel to Heavenly Father when we cannot speak.

Doug Addison speaks of a heavenly encounter where he saw books with the recorded prayers of mothers and women. He read Psalms 56, where he saw millions of books of unanswered prayer. While he was wondering how all of these could ever be answered, the Lord suddenly called angels to come and take the books to another section of Heaven that had the person's calling or anointing in that section.

The Lord then told Doug to watch for the answers to those prayers to start coming, though it may look differently than expected. He said that many women had sown in tears and are about to reap joy and be promoted with new authority. Then an angel carrying a golden scroll of the names of women who are about to be honored appeared. He experienced this on Mother's Day of 2017, and later that year injustices against women began being exposed at a whole new level. The Lord was answering prayers and women were being promoted.

With this type of promotion, the Books of Justice get opened, and where there were injustices, the books are about to get balanced. We continue to see injustices exposed at unprecedented levels and repayment made on their behalf. He mentioned there are similar sections for men, too.

Here is another confirmation of the importance of these books in Heaven. I was especially blessed knowing that unanswered prayers are kept in a storehouse until the time to be released. It is encouraging to know that our tears and prayers are so precious to the Lord that He keeps them in a special treasury room. The whole message was inspiring. You can listen in its entirety[8].

My challenging season led me to learn about the Courtrooms of Heaven. Did you know that the Bible is full of legal language such as our Father as Judge, Yeshua as Advocate, Holy Spirit as Counselor, and Satan as our Accuser? Robert Henderson and Praying Medic[9] have great teachings and understanding on this topic that I would highly recommend for further insight.

There are times when prayers go unanswered due to a legal issue. Just like here, if there is a legitimate accusation against us and we fail to show up for Court to answer those accusations, we automatically lose. It is the same in the Courts of Heaven. Job 1, Daniel 10, Zechariah 3, Revelation 12:10 are a few examples of the Courts of Heaven.

So what Dennis saw in the archives of tears proves that they are kept for trial. How encouraging to know there will be justice.

To confirm this aspect even further, I heard an interview with Tanner Searle, a counselor, as she shared about her journey. She had been in a difficult season and crying out to the Lord, as many of us do, "Where are You, God? I'm barely hanging on…I can't do this much longer…there is so much pain…why are You doing nothing about this?" She added that this is the logical reasoning process of the left brain which trauma causes to get muddled.

She saw Father as Judge come to her with His hand near His heart and drew out a vial that He held towards the enemy in the Court of Heaven. He revealed that this was evidence presented into the Court system. It was her tears that He was holding near to His heart, and was the reason why the enemy deserved to be convicted.

He is the Accuser (Rev.12:10), and we can bring litigation and legislation against him since he is defeated, but he is also a legalist. Here is evidence of him breaking the laws of love, bringing pain, trauma, loss, etc., throughout our lives and bloodlines.

It is comforting to know that we can experience justice now. We do not have to wait until death or "someday" as our loving Father created a system where we can adjudicate justice on behalf of ourselves and others for the wrongs done to us since the beginning.

The sense of injustice that we feel is even a legal term. We have inherently received this from our Father in Heaven, Who did everything that He could legally to set us free. It is now up to us to accept and apply it to our lives in the Courtrooms of Heaven to see justice manifested on earth as in Heaven.

In 2018, Justify the horse became the second undefeated horse to win the Triple Crown 45 years to the day of when Secretariat won it. Justify means to administer justice. Isn't it fitting that we can now see the manifestation in our lives of what happened 2000 years ago? We are justified.

I included a sample Court of Heaven session in Chapter Ten to use as a guideline.

CHAPTER FIVE

Intercessory Tears

A Scripture that speaks to the intercessory part of our tears is Romans 8:26-27 (CJV):

Similarly, the Spirit helps us in our weakness; for we don't know how to pray the way we should. But the Spirit himself pleads on our behalf with groanings too deep for words; and the one who searches hearts knows exactly what the Spirit is thinking because his pleadings for God's people accord with God's will.

There are times in prayer when no words can come— only tears and groaning from deep within our spirit— one with Holy Spirit.

According to 1 Corinthians 6:20 (TPT), Yeshua sweat great drops of blood. *You were God's expensive purchase, paid for with tears of blood.*

Could that have been his body's way of shedding tears? It was such an enormous burden that He was carrying— one that none of us can fully understand apart from revelation. He felt all of the sin, grief, shame, and pain from every human being ever created.

When I think of the times that the pain and grief I was carrying was nearly unbearable, I try to imagine what He must have felt, and it brings me to humble thanksgiving and praise.

Isaiah 53 describes Him as a "man of sorrows, acquainted with grief." How comforting to know there is One who understands and knows, as well as felt every painful emotion and event that we have. How amazing is that? He is the ultimate intercessor of all time. The term intercessor means "to stand in the gap." It is a term used for those who pray on behalf of another. Yeshua, our Messiah, took our place on the Cross of Calvary. He took what we deserved as punishment, so we can now partake of what He deserves in blessings as a joint-heir (Romans 8; Ephesians 2).

Isaiah 53:3 (EXB)

He was hated [despised] and rejected by people. He had much pain [A man of pain/suffering/sorrows] and suffering [one who knew/was acquainted with pain/grief]. People would not even look at [turned their backs on; hid their faces from] him. He was hated [despised], and we didn't even notice him [or did not esteem him].

Hebrews 7:25 (AMP) tells us that Yeshua is still interceding for us. *Therefore He is able also to save to the uttermost (completely, perfectly, finally, and for all time and eternity) those who come to God through Him, since He is always living to make petition to God and intercede with Him and intervene for them.*

Yeshua was no stranger to tears, pain, or grief. He knew and suffered from all of it. The shortest verse in the Bible is John 11:35,

Yeshua wept.

I am curious as to what those tears looked like under the microscope. What would they tell us about what He felt and what each tear represented?

I have heard various interpretations of why people think He wept, but what would it be like to actually see His tears under a microscope and know for sure? Somehow I think perhaps each one carried what each of ours carries. After all, if He took all of our sin, grief, sickness, and disease; maybe He was able to carry each one of our tears and their record within His as well.

Yeshua said that we are to be the salt of the earth, but if we lose our flavor then we will not make an impact. Interestingly, along with our tears, blood also contains salt. Could His great drops of blood mentioned in 1 Corinthians 6 have been part of His intercessory cry? Perhaps…

Leviticus states that life is in the blood. I believe that's why the enemy takes such pleasure in the shedding of innocent blood. Blood is a doorway into the spirit world; whether it be through the old covenant sacrifices or occult practices which are a twisted counterfeit of the original. That is why the ultimate blood sacrifice made way for us to go boldly through the Door Himself to the Throne of Grace (Hebrews 4:16). We now have instant access without having to go through ancient rituals — the veil of separation supernaturally torn from top to bottom.

Blood holds the record of our DNA, including that of our ancestors. Besides our hair color, body shape, and personality traits, this is where generational iniquity is recorded, which is a root cause of things like disease, trauma, addictions, etc. Science has found that when someone receives a bone marrow transplant, their actual DNA changes as they begin taking on the donor's, which is why bodies will reject it.

I know someone who received the heart of a young man killed in an accident. After that, he was fearful while driving in a car, which had not happened before. So he took on the trauma of what that young donor experienced as he died, as it was recorded in his DNA.

As I pray for people now— especially in the Courts of Heaven, I apply the blood of Yeshua to their DNA, erasing the record against them since His blood speaks a better word than that of Abel's, and deletes the handwriting of ordinances against them, (Colossians 1:14; Hebrews 12:24). I often have us take communion together at the end of ministry or a Court session applying Yeshua's blood to our DNA to cleanse and change it.

I heard testimony from a woman who had been taking communion regularly and doing this. When she had a blood test, none of her DNA markers were there as the record of her genetic code had been cleansed and erased. That is what the finished work of the Cross is all about.

I believe His blood is also enough to heal the soul wounds caused by traumatic events throughout our bloodlines up to us, precipitating events that resulted in much grief and sorrow. I know, because I have seen it work. We now have a better understanding of ancient truths, enabling us to overcome here on earth AS IT IS IN HEAVEN!

John 10:10 (TLV)

The thief comes only to steal, slaughter, and destroy. I have come that they might have life, and have it abundantly!

His will for our lives here and now is to have an abundant one. If we wait until Heaven, then death becomes our savior instead of Yeshua. Wherever anything has the fingerprints of Satan, that is not His will for our lives. Yes, He can and does use it for our good and His glory as we learn and grow through these circumstances and events.

Colossians 1:19-20 (TLV)

He is the beginning, the firstborn from the dead— so that He might come to have first place in all things. 19 For God was pleased to have all His fullness dwell in Him 20 and through Him to reconcile all things to Himself, making peace through the blood of His cross— whether things on earth or things in heaven!

The purpose of His life, death, resurrection, and ascension was to reconcile us to our Heavenly Father. One day as I was reading this chapter, Holy Spirit asked me if I saw that fully manifested. Then went on to show me how that part was now up to us as co-heirs with Yeshua. He did His part, and now wants to partner with us to see the full restoration of ALL things!

All of creation is waiting for us to set it free from their captivity— for us to mature as sons of the Most High since we are adopted. Sadly, our concept of adoption is usually with images of poor, rejected, homeless children, begging for help. I am excited to see how this next generation is learning to celebrate adoption with, Gotch-ya Days! I have watched the thrill of the family and community coming together to help financially, along with the subsequent celebrations. Did you know that in the USA an adopted child can never be disinherited? This is not so with natural children, only with the adopted. Now that's the picture of our adoption into the Family of Heaven we are to have.

We are already seated in Messiah as born-again believers. The wages of sin is death, and Yeshua paid the ultimate blood sacrificial price. Therefore, He shares what He has with us in this new covenant relationship. I submit to you that we do not have to accept these horrible things as part of Father's will for us. I see that as still tied to old covenant thinking and fatalism.

While He is most definitely sovereign, He has also given us a free will—true love can only come from having the choice.

There are consequences to our choices, as well as the law of sowing and reaping that come into play. Too often He is blamed for things that are a product of our choices—even generationally, which the enemy then has a legal right to bring against us until we address it in the Courts of Heaven. This understanding has changed my view of Him and my prayer life.

Allow me to break this down a bit more. Say I climb a tree and purposely jump out of it and break my legs. Was that the will of Yahweh? Or, since I have a free will and decided to do it, merely a matter of the law of gravity along with the law of sowing and reaping in effect? I believe the latter.

Yeshua paid the ultimate price, but it is now up to us to apply it to the accusations. The Bible says that He was slain before the foundations of the world formed and we died with Him. So why did He need to come and go through it again? Perhaps because we needed to have evidence of what had already taken place, and since spiritual things are outside of the boundaries of time and space, we can step into that and apply it to each incidence in our lives including our bloodline.

So why go through all of the steps to doing so? Maybe for us to fully appreciate everything done for us. Each time I go through inner healing, Courts of Heaven, etc., I am that much more thankful as I receive an increased revelation of the price Yeshua paid, and it causes me to fall deeper in love with Him and have greater thanksgiving and praise!

Yeshua claimed that the enemy of this world had nothing in common in Him.

John 14:30 (AMPC),

"I will not talk with you much more, for the prince, evil genius ruler of the world is coming. And he has no claim on Me. He has nothing in common with Me; there is nothing in Me that belongs to him, and he has no power over Me."

There was nothing in His mind, will, emotions, or DNA that belonged to or was in common with Satan; therefore he had no dominion over Him. In verse 12 of John 14, Yeshua said that those who believe in Him would do the works He did, and even *greater works* because He was going to the Father. Since He took the keys of death, hell, and the grave back from Satan that Adam had forfeited, we no longer have to be subjected to those things as we apply the finished work of the Cross and allow Yeshua's blood to speak on our behalf through repentance, forgiveness, and healing.

In the old covenant on Yom Kippur, two goats were selected; one was sacrificed for sin and the other taking the sins of the people as the priest laid hands on it and set it free—the scapegoat (Lev. 16:10). Yeshua did both. 1 John 1:9 says that if we confess our sins, He is faithful and just to forgive and cleanse us of all unrighteousness. That is how He answered for both goats. We have authority over the enemy and everything we need to be victorious here and now.

He does use all of these things in our lives to make something beautiful out of them as Romans 8:28 says. I have experienced this first hand. The trials and difficulties were used to refine me and draw me deeper into Him, His written Word, and to achieve the abundant life here and now He promised us. However, I do not believe that He is in control, as He is not controlling, but I do think that He is ultimately the One in charge. All was taken care of through the Cross of Calvary, His death, resurrection, and ascension, where we are now seated with and in Him in heavenly places (Romans 8; Ephesians 1-2). This is the Great Exchange which happened at Calvary that we can apply at any time. We will go further into this during the Court of Heaven session in Chapter Ten.

1 Cor 6:19-20 (TLV)

Have you forgotten that your body is now the sacred temple of the Spirit of Holiness, who lives in you? You don't belong to yourself any longer, for the gift of God, the Holy Spirit, lives inside your sanctuary. You were God's expensive purchase, paid for with <u>tears of blood</u> (as translated from the Aramaic), so by all means, then, use your body to bring glory to God!

CHAPTER SIX

Gates of Pearl

Pearls form through a long process. The oyster has two shells, each having a protective layer covering the organ that keeps it alive.

The pearls form as a response to an irritant such as sand. When this happens, the oyster produces a protective coating known as mother-of-pearl which helps reduce the irritation. This coating consists of microscopic crystals of calcium carbonate which also lines the interior of the shells. The layers of mother-of-pearl coat the irritant, eventually forming the pearl.

The salt in the calcium carbonate is used in supplements for bone and heart health and is what keeps the oyster's outer coating strong.

I see the connection in our lives with tears and pearls— emotions of weakness with strength coating those tears. Could it be that shedding tears helps to strengthen us within? Is this to protect our organs the same way mother-of-pearl is produced to protect the organs of the oyster? If that was not wonderful enough, our Creator saw fit to make it a beautiful process with a reward at the end— a pearl!

Job 28:17-18 (CJB)

Neither gold nor glass can be compared with it; nor can it be exchanged for a bowl of fine gold, let alone coral or crystal; for indeed, the price of wisdom is above that of pearls.

May we indeed treasure our pearls of wisdom gained through life's experiences.

Looking back to the liquid pearl, or as we have just discovered, mother-of-pearl, reminds me of a message from Bill Johnson, pastor of Bethel Church in Redding, CA. He spoke of the Twelve Gates of Pearl referred to in Revelation 21:21, as being connected with Gates of Praise (Ps. 100:4; Isaiah 60:18). When we praise Him in the midst of difficulties, we are erecting these Gates of Pearl.

Since pearls form through irritation, it is through times of hope deferred, loss, grief, disappointment, etc., when we decide to praise Him in spite of, and in the midst of the pain and difficulties, that we are building these Gates of Pearl. It is easy to praise Him and declare His goodness when all is going well and our way; but the sacrifice of praise comes when we do so in the midst of things not going our way, yet praise Him anyway. Each time we do so, we are adding pearl to the Gate of Praise. Think about it for a moment. If each gate is made up of a SINGLE PEARL— how must that look! Are they portals made of mother-of-pearl? One could mediate on that for a while.

Some Bible commentaries speak of pearls holding the highest rank among precious stones in ancient times. It is also the only gem in which man cannot improve upon with his skills, unlike other gemstones.

The Latin term unio (unity) was applied to the pearl because no two were found precisely alike. Just like us, and like our tears.

Messiah is known as the Gate and Pearl of Great Price. Therefore, we enter all things through Him and His finished work as we are one with and in Him.

The Man of Sorrows acquainted with grief treasures each one of our tears and places them in a bottle. These are trophies and reminders of the sorrows caused through the fall of humanity and powers of hell. Our hope is in Him, and the fact that not one of our tears will be forgotten or shed in vain because He keeps them along with their record. The intercession of Yeshua, along with our intercessory prayers, are the seeds sown that will reap a great harvest of joy.

Psalm 126:4-6 (NLV)

Bring back our people, O Lord, like the rivers in the South. Those who plant with tears will gather fruit with songs of joy. He who goes out crying as he carries his bag of seed will return with songs of joy as he brings much grain with him.

Psalm 126:4-6 (NLV)

Bring back our people, O Lord, like the rivers in the South. Those who plant with tears will gather fruit with songs of joy. He who goes out crying as he carries his bag of seed will return with songs of joy as he brings much grain with him.

Psalms 30:5, 11-12 (NLV & NLT)

Crying may last for a night, but joy comes with the new day. You have turned my crying into joyful dancing. You have taken away my clothes of mourning and clothed me with joy, that I might sing praises to you and not be silent. O Lord my God, I will give you thanks forever!

Joey Le Tourneau[10] had a precious word regarding tears on The Elijah List that beautifully sums it up:

Praise Him in the process and allow yourself to know just how personal you are to Him. Receive the tears that He weeps on your behalf, weeping because you, one He loves so dearly, feeling the pain of answers and hope deferred. He feels the same pain. He bears it with you to the point of tears. And He uses those tears as His intercession on your behalf, loving you to the point of resurrection and life that waits on the other side.

Prov. 13:12 (TLV)

Hope deferred makes the heart sick, but longing fulfilled is a tree of life.

CHAPTER SEVEN

Grieving is Good

Crying was considered a sign of weakness in the culture where I grew up. Many cultures have adopted this mentality, and I have to wonder, why? Have we been robbed of the healthy way to process the loss of someone we love or other forms of loss, grief or other emotions?

Since we are created in the image of our Father, let's break this down a bit more. Our brains are separated into the right and left hemispheres. The right-brain is where creativity, spiritual gifts, and emotions are activated. The left side is where logic, language, and things like mathematics process. We need both. Babies have very active right brains, but western education indoctrinates them out of it into the left-brain analysis. It seems if that happens too soon, it can hinder healthy emotional growth. Cultures with both sides of the brain activated appear to thrive much better.

Church culture has become very Greek, therefore under the influence of stoicism—to not display emotions. However, the Apostle Paul wrote to the Roman believers to weep with those who weep, so why do we try to stop it? Why do we consider it as weakness? How often have we heard, "just be strong," knowing that it really meant to not show emotion as if it was a sign of strength.

The New Testament was translated from the Greek, so one has to wonder how much was lost or changed that has influenced us and our feelings. Yeshua was Hebrew which is a very different culture and language. They think more in circles rather than linearly. Merely looking at the cycles of Jewish feasts helps to illustrate that as they are cyclical.

As a missionary, I learned about hot and cold cultures. The hot cultures are more emotional with the cold cultures being more logical or linear in their thinking. A good example is to think of someone from Latin America compared to someone from Northern Europe. Even the foods from these regions attest to the "hot and cold" theory. It was important for me to understand which culture I was addressing when I taught. If I went to a culture that was more circular or right-brain in their learning, then doing a typical, "A B C—1 2 3" didn't work with them as they would get lost and bored. Storytelling and the use of visuals is the best way to learn, as well as life experiences which are more right-brain activities. How did Yeshua teach? He used a lot of storytelling, also known as parables, along with life experiences which included signs, wonders, and miracles.

Let's go back to Dr. Joseph Stromberg's study of tears where he mentions that emotional tears have protein-based hormones, which are natural painkillers released when we are stressed. In His wisdom, our Creator saw fit to bless us with this natural painkiller and stress reducer, even before the fall of humanity. Why then, do so many of us still struggle with showing that type of emotion? Can we give ourselves and others permission to cry and release emotion? If not, why?

We will now look at how the Jewish culture handles the death of a loved one. The first three days are for the mourners to cry and mourn the loss. Visitors are not encouraged to begin speaking to the mourners until the mourners start to talk. It is considered a proper action for the mourner to cry and weep as they remember the good things about the deceased. Efforts to comfort them should not be made to stop the crying, but to bring out the good qualities in the deceased. Comforting is made by sympathizing with their loss and encouraging them to speak out their experiences.

The first three days that a mourner sits "shiva" is generally focused on the deceased person, whereas the last four days, the focus shifts to the mourner re-entering the world. There is a gradual and natural shift of moving from the loss to the adjustment.

I have seen some cultures wail as they grieve, then once that time is over, they go on. Are we doing ourselves a disservice by holding back the tears?

Ps 84: *Valley of Baca* (weeping)

The medical community is discovering the adverse effects on our bodies by trapped emotions. I have learned through my involvement with essential oils how the frequencies from these oils penetrate the blood-brain barrier where memories and emotions are stored. Our Creator had that in mind when He created the plants before humanity— with His breath!

Creation carries the sound and frequencies of His voice, and each plant, tree, etc., have specific healing properties for which He designed them to have. Essential oils are the distilled form of these which are concentrated and work with the body's frequencies and our intentions. Our soul is made up of our mind, will, and emotions. Our will can determine if we allow those trapped memories or emotions to be released or not. Holy Spirit will not overstep our will. Therefore, when using specific essential oils, they can assist in unblocking memories and emotions stored up— if we are open to it.

Toxic thoughts and emotions are known to have adverse effects on our whole being. Dr. Caroline Leaf, a top neuroscientist who is a Christian, has a lot of great material on this that I recommend. Our triune self: spirit, soul, and body are all connected and therefore affected.

1 Thessalonians 5:23 (TLV)

Now may the God of shalom Himself make you completely holy; and may your whole spirit and soul and body be kept complete, blameless at the coming of our Lord Yeshua the Messiah.

If our Creator gave us emotions and the ability to show them as He does, why do we resist them? Who told us it was a sign of weakness? Since it is our body's way of being able to release emotions, toxins, and generally cleanse us, perhaps knowing this can help us learn to honor our feelings and that of others. Let's permit ourselves to release them. As the Body of Messiah, to come out of the stoicism that has permeated the church age and learn to honor and care for our emotions and that of others in the way He intended.

One of the adverse effects of not crying according to Stephen Sideroff, Ph.D., a staff psychologist at Santa Monica University of California Los Angeles & Orthopaedic Hospital and clinical director of the Moonview Treatment Center in Santa Monica, CA., is that it may lead to depression.[11] "Those who suppress emotions and cannot cry may be jeopardizing their physical health," Jodi DeLuca, Ph.D., a neuropsychologist at Tampa General Hospital in Florida, agrees. She cites a saying attributed to British psychiatrist Henry Maudsley, among others:

'The sorrow which has no vent in tears may make other organs weep.'

Could it be that as people age and have health issues, that much of it could be prevented by merely dealing with unresolved and trapped emotions?

The soul is a beautiful gift to us. It contains our mind, will, and emotions. When we do not handle our emotions properly, they must go somewhere. The medical community has proven how bitterness and unforgiveness connect with cancer. It is an outward picture of what is happening in the soul. It eats away, and when it does not have an outlet, the body begins to turn on itself. Grief seems to have the effect of weakening the lungs.

I find it interesting that there are so many autoimmune diseases, which is basically the body turning on itself, and much of it can be traced back to trauma, grief, unforgiveness, bitterness— all emotionally related and left alone.

Sometimes we need to know that we have permission to grieve, to be angry, and then deal with it.

Often Christian culture frowns on any show of anger; even though the Bible says in Ephesians 4:26 to be angry, but not sin. In other words, acknowledge the anger and what is causing it, then deal with it before it takes over and turns into sin. It goes on to say not to let the sun go down on it. It is essential to take care of it immediately. I consider this healthcare and dis-ease prevention prescribed by our Father. Indeed an affordable care act!

Denial is another one of our enemies. I have sadly seen its effects on many people. Emotions are not necessarily a sign of weakness, but that we have loved, lived, and lost. We have lived life outside of a secured fortress and risked all it has to offer.

It speaks to crushed dreams, lost hope, and overwhelming disappointment. The unspoken prayers too deep for words It also speaks of the tenderness of heart open to love, sharing other's hurt and joy along with our own. Yet, we continue living. We allow ourselves a moment in time to memorialize all of our losses by allowing them to squeeze out through liquid pearls. Alas, none lost, but each captured and stored in a heavenly archive with the record of their cause.

Beautifully, along with those tears are those of joy and happiness when a desire long forgot is fulfilled. Seeing the answers to prayers never spoken, dreams too deep to hope for come to pass with unspeakable joy running, streaming down into a river of life. Even those have their vials in Heaven's archives of life. Oh, the stories each one of these hold. Why hold them back when each is a pearl of great price? Celebrate and see them as the precious jewels that they are.

Taking Action:

If you relate to not allowing yourself to show emotion—perhaps you have either knowingly or unknowingly made a vow never to show emotions, etc., then please take a moment and pray through the following:

Father, on behalf of myself, my bloodline, culture, and church culture, all the way to the beginning with You—— I change my mind (repent) and ask forgiveness for every time that I/we have spoken, thought, or been in agreement that showing emotion(s) is a sign of weakness. Where I/we have judged others for showing emotion and judged them as weak, I ask that You would forgive me/us. I forgive my bloodline ancestors, the church, my culture, and those in my life who taught me that showing emotion was a sign of weakness, and I ask that You would, too.

I acknowledge that we have denied the emotions in which You, Father, have given to us as a gift. I now change my mind about that—along with the vows, words, and judgments that, "I won't cry," or "I will never show emotion or any weakness," or "those who do are weak or pathetic," "it's not safe to cry," etc, (fill in what most applies to you_____) and all of the adverse effects that it has had on my health and relationships.

(Take a moment and allow for any/all other accusations against you and your bloodline to come forth. It can occur as a thought, memory, something you see, feel, or hear. Be as thorough as necessary. You can always come back and repeat if you remember something at a later time).

I ask for Divorce Papers from Stoicism, Showing Emotions is a Sign of Weakness and everything connected with it, whether it is in my conscious, subconscious, or unconscious self, in my bloodline, and as a Christian all the way back to You. I ask that You forgive me/us for judging others who do show emotion as being weak, and confess that attitude as prideful, as well as judging something that You created as "good" to be something not good. I give you permission to awaken and release my emotions and teach me how to handle them healthily. As a follower of Yeshua, to be an example of how to show emotions and to allow others to do so. I ask for both sides of my brain to work in harmony with one another.

I forgive those who have used emotions against me or others around me as a means of manipulation or control and ask that You would, too. Where I have developed the mindset that those showing emotions were trying to control or manipulate, or saw them as unstable, please forgive me.

I ask for Your forgiveness, cleansing, and healing from the effects of this sin, vow, and trauma, as I put these things to death by nailing them to Yeshua's Cross. I include all agreements, lies, oaths, covenants, pledges, contracts, curses, bitter root judgments and expectations, promises that I and my bloodline have made with this, along with every familiar spirit, their underlings, and all entities connected. I cover them with Yeshua's blood which erases all record of it. From this point on, may His blood answer for any accusations confessed.

And on every altar in every dimension where our names were traded upon, I apply Yeshua's blood and ask that angels be released to smash and utterly destroy any remaining altar or record of these things. I ask that You remove every hook, devise, tuning fork, implant, or magnet attached to me.

By faith, I receive Your forgiveness, cleansing, and healing into my body, soul, and spirit—every part of me and my DNA. I invite You to come and take these things out of my soul, body, and head as You heal the memory and effects of the sin and trauma—I give them to You, and ask that You replace them with (insert what you would like replaced with—love, peace, acceptance, tenderness, ability to show emotions, etc.).

Since repentance means to turn the other direction, I now see the value in tears and emotions, and from this moment onward, I will allow them and no longer hold them back. I will also allow others to freely express them without trying to make them stop due to any feelings of discomfort.

I am thankful to You for holding every one of my tears in my bottle along with their record book. Thank You for tears and for all emotions being released and the honor of feeling as You do, since I am made in Your image. Thank You for enabling me to handle them in a healthy way. I gratefully receive the divorce papers from this. May they be released on earth as in the Courtroom of Heaven, with the angels archiving them as they release them on earth. Thank You for this precious gift of freedom!

CHAPTER EIGHT

Hope

Throughout these difficult years when I received the word regarding the vial of liquid pearl, the Lord kept speaking hope to me. In Chapter Two, I mentioned my return journey to Texas beginning on the Highway of Hope through Hope, AR. to staying in the "The Hope Room" at my friend's house, then later living near "New Hope" road. It was an ongoing theme for some time as I learned to hope again.

I looked up some of the Hebrew names and meanings for Hope, and came across Isaiah 40:31, which I had always known to say, *"they that wait upon the Lord,"* but began seeing, *"those who hope in the Lord will renew their strength."*

Here are two of the original Hebrew words and definitions for wait that I found:

Strong's #6960 **qavah**: to bind together, twisting like a rope; to look patiently for, tarry, wait, **hope.**

Strong's #2342 **chuwl**: to twist or twirl (in a circular or spiral manner), specifically to dance. To writhe in pain like childbirth, to wait, make to bring forth, fall grievously with pain, grieve, **hope,** rest...were among some of the ways this word is used.

Notice the words that describe waiting/hoping in the Lord that include; writhing in pain, grieving— but also, rest, hope, wait, along with dancing?

He has turned my mourning into dancing. Psalms 30

I painted on paper what I imagined as I meditated on these two definitions. It is a divine dance that is sometimes painful, but like an entangling, or tango with our DNA together. I began with primary colors swirling, then when mixed became a whole new color.

These two words alone bring together the verses referring to sowing in tears and reaping joy; it is dancing when the thing waited for comes forth. Though we cry in the night time of our lives, joy and dancing come in the morning. What a beautiful description of what happens with our many forms of tears and how they bring forth something so beautiful!

Each one is so precious, carrying with it the emotion and intention within. Not one is wasted, but kept in a bottle along with the prayers and tears of Yeshua, bringing forth answers to even the deepest prayers which go beyond words and can only come in the form of tears.

As we wait and hope in Him, is this beautiful picture of entangling ourselves with Him in a Divine Tango of two lovers becoming one, with our most profound pain and travailing prayers— tears and deep groans that the Spirit within us helps us to express (Romans 8:26-27).

Our hope comes from the fact that no matter the most profound pain, grief, sorrow, or disappointment that only tears can express; with Messiah, we will dance and experience joy! Though Hope deferred may have made our hearts sick, with the longing fulfilled, it is a tree of life (Prov. 13:12). He is our Hope. Therefore, no matter what we face, there is always Hope. Hope in Him, as He is our all in all.

I had a spiritual encounter with the Lord giving me a pair of teardrop earrings made out of crystal. When I asked Him about it, He said they were my trophies carrying the record of my tears. He was honoring me and letting me know how precious they were to Him, and wearing them on my ears was to be a reminder of what I have sown. My sense was to be encouraged and not lose hope since they crystallized like salt, which of course is one of the compounds found in tears.

I want to conclude this book by letting you know that even though I shared parts of my darkest seasons and events with you, He has been faithful to provide in marvelous and miraculous ways and has used many people and friends as vehicles of blessing.

The first year and a half back in Houston I stayed in my friend's beautiful apartment. One of the difficult things I left in Germany were my dishes. I had collected them over the years, friends had blessed me with pieces for my birthday, Christmas, etc., so they held a special place in my heart. While staying in my friend's apartment, the dishes I used there were very similar. I took that as a wink and nod from my Father that He knew the most intimate places and desires of my heart. He was with me in this challenging place.

I am thankful that He led me on the journey of beginning my day with thanksgiving and praise (Ps. 100:4). That helped me in the direst of circumstances to be thankful for the smallest things. To meditate on His character and nature, to magnify those things and remain grateful. It wasn't denying my circumstances, but submitting them into His hands and letting go as much as I knew how to, and changing my focus. Each miracle and blessing brought tears of joy, thanksgiving, praise, and love for Him knowing that He was caring for me through this dark time. The refiner's fire has done a profound work, and those areas where the enemy used to have a landing place, he no longer does. I am healthier and more peaceful even in challenging circumstances as I continue on this journey.

Hope my friend. Hope in Him. Cast your cares and burdens upon Him because He does love and care for you so very much. Though your weeping, travailing tears may have been for a very long and challenging night, hang onto Him. Morning is coming and with it the dance of your life with the Love of your life!

You will laugh again, you will have joy, and as you praise Him in the midst of the darkness of despair and disappointment while journeying through the valley of death, beautiful pearls are being created giving you entrance before Your King! Remember, you are walking through the valley of weeping as He is bringing you to the door of hope, and it is only a shadow of death. He has a table prepared for you to sit with Him and rest as you taste and see His goodness. You will get through this as it becomes a spring for you. Nothing wasted, all extremely precious to Him and recorded in His book and bottles.

Hosea 2:15-16 (AMP)

"Then I will give her her vineyards from there,
And make the Valley of Achor (Trouble) a door of hope
and expectation [anticipating the time when I will restore
My favor on her].
And she will sing there and respond as in the days
of her youth
As in the day when she came up from the land of Egypt.
"It shall come about in that day," says the Lord,
"That you will call Me Ishi (my husband)
And will no longer call Me Baali (my Baal)."

Song of Solomon 8:5 (AMP)

"Who is this coming up from the wilderness Leaning
upon her beloved?"

Prayer:

Father, I thank You that in the midst of everything, You are my anchor of hope. Thank You for tears which bring healing, release, comfort, and cleansing. I place my hope in You that does not disappoint. Though I don't understand all things, I trust You. I intertwine/qavah myself with You, becoming one with You. Heal the places in my heart that need it. I receive Your comfort and strength. Thank You for the work You are doing— though mourning has lasted for a very long night, I know that joy is coming in the morning. In the meantime, I am Yours, and I love You.

Romans 15:13 (TLV)

Now may the God of hope fill you with all joy and shalom in trusting, so you may overflow with hope in the power of the Ruach ha-Kodesh.

CHAPTER NINE

Trauma

Trauma Addressed in the Courts of Heaven

Trauma is a shocking event that is either physical or emotional, experienced or witnessed with the record of it embedded into our DNA and memory. We also carry the memory of trauma that our ancestors experienced. Examples include those with fears or phobias of things such as spiders, heights, water, dogs, etc. when they have never experienced any events which would logically explain those fears. Due to the nature of trauma, the shock of it can open one up to spiritual oppression which can then cause the person and their bloodline to continue to experience similar wounds until addressed legally and healed by Yeshua's blood.

It is for this reason that I have included this prayer. Some have found instant freedom and relief after praying through it. Using essential oils such as frankincense by inhaling and applying to the back of the head where the emotions and memories reside can assist in this process.

Father, I repent (change my mind) for my response to and acceptance of any trauma witnessed or experienced throughout my generations as well as my own life. I recognize and acknowledge that trauma is not of You, Father, so I want to remove its impact and influence in every form and dimension.

On behalf of myself and bloodline all the way back to You and forward into future generations, I forgive (each) _____ (person, leader, authority figure, business, organization, ministry, etc.) who has been a participant, agreed to, or associated with each trauma encountered and I ask You to do the same. I forgive and release all that has taken place from the past into the present. I also forgive and release all that has affected my and/or _____'s future.

For all trauma witnessed and experienced through the five physical gates of my body, I release the following:

All sounds and their frequencies, including the triggers associated with each one.

All visual imprints and the triggers associated with each one.

All aromas captured and the triggers associated with each traumatic experience.

All perceptions and sensations experienced with the tongue and associated triggers.

All physical contact and perceptions, including the triggers associated with each trauma.

All trauma experienced or witnessed through any receptors before, during, or after all traumatic events— embedded or blocked from my memory, are now released to You, Father.

I release all of the impacts of trauma whether it was induced by:

Earthly events: *(flood, fire, tornado, hurricane, earthquake, etc.)*.

Loss: *(death, divorce, miscarriage, financial, home, health, business, finances, etc.)*.

Tragedy: *(accidents, explosion, terrorism, war, etc.)*.

At the hands of others: *(betrayal, abuse, rape, incest, occultic, satanic, masonic, programming, torture, etc.)*.

Self: *(substance abuse, addictions, abortion, surgery, cutting, masochist/self-inflicted injury, realized self-sabotage, realized truth, etc.)*.

I now place into Your hands the following manifestations of trauma that I have agreed to or participated in: *toxic emotions, toxic perceptions, toxic mindsets, toxic reactions, toxic beliefs, and toxic responses.*

I surrender the symptoms of trauma: *being easily and frequently stressed out, hyper-vigilance, extreme sensitivity. I now place in Your hands the following manifestations of trauma that I have agreed to or participated in: toxic emotions, toxic perceptions, toxic mindsets, toxic reactions, toxic beliefs, and toxic responses.*

I relinquish the symptoms of trauma: *being easily and frequently stressed out, hyper-vigilance, extreme sensitivity to light and sound, muscles that refuse to fully relax, flashbacks, exaggerated emotional and startled responses, intrusive imagery, exaggerated or diminished sexual activity, nightmares, panic attacks, shame, denial, avoidance behaviors, freezing in fear as nervous or "negative" emotions rise, feeling helpless, amnesia, forgetfulness, inability to make commitments, chronic fatigue, issues with my immune system, endocrine dysfunction, (ex. problems with glands, pancreas, hormones & reproductive organs), neck and back problems, digestive issues, spastic colon, severe PMS, asthma, depression, feelings of alienation, detachment, and inability to love/nurture/bond with another.*

<u>I hand to You my battles with</u>: *anger, rage, rejection, self hatred, owning responsibility, apathy, self pity, despair, depression, fractured focus or memory, any illness or disease, heightened nervous system, unable to relax, phantom/chronic and/or acute pain, self sabotage, self centeredness, control, manipulation, bullying, domination, deceit, abuse in all forms, victim mentality, masturbation, porn and/ or other exaggerated sexual activity, substance abuse, all types of fear, unrealized expectations, unmet needs, unresolved issues.*

I renounce all agreements, covenants, contracts, participation and association with every aspect of trauma already indicated. I ask that the records of these items be expunged. I apply this to myself, the land and time it took place, and in every dimension, realm, and timeline, that all aspects would no longer be tied or defiled but whole and clean back through time, no longer holding the record of these events.

I ask Your forgiveness for any spoken words tied to any trauma experienced or witnessed throughout my generations. Whether the words were in the form of an oath, a vow, a curse, or promise. I nail each one to the Cross of Yeshua along with all entities connected and cover them with His blood. I do this on behalf of myself and each one in my generational line backward and forwards to future generations. I renounce agreements, participation, and association with each occurrence and revoke all rights.

I implore the Court that all traumatic memories and their triggers in my soul and DNA be cleansed of all negative emotions and energies so the events going forward will merely be facts in a history book. Upon granting this, I, nor my family will experience any backlash, retaliation, be haunted or held in bondage. As these frequencies are being removed, that there no longer be any magnets, hooks, thorns, tuning forks, implants, booby traps, devices or programming of any kind in any dimension in operation to attract future trauma.

I request an injunction against all trauma, and an overturning of all evil documents to remove my family and me from any future harm. I recognize that being hurt is short term while trauma intends to bring permanent damage.

May all structures and booby traps be dismantled and removed. Structures that have resulted in barely surviving, escapism, the erection of internal walls for protection, multiple personalities, all programming, the adoption of false identities, false security, performance mindsets, control, false authority, apathy, passivity, passive aggression, along with any other false structure.

By faith, I receive Your forgiveness, cleansing, and healing by the blood of Yeshua from the effects of trauma and the memory associated with it into my DNA, my soul, and my body. May Your frequencies come and realign every part of me including every one of my gateways to their original function, purpose, and blueprint design with Your holy fire, living water, and a heavenly gold covering over my family and me.

I declare that I am a spirit, with a soul, living in a fleshly body as this is the correct order of being created in the image of my Father and Brother in Heaven. I look forward to the physical manifestations of a restored mind and body in every way.

I request divorce papers for everything addressed in the Court today with a copy of the injunction against trauma, as well as an overturning of all evil documents connected with trauma. I receive these from the Court, and I thank You.

As I place each of these papers in my belly, I own the transformation of all that has been made available through this Court session. Thank You, Father, for teaching me all of what this entails and how to live this model of Heaven on Earth.

I seal all of this on every timeline, age, dimension, and realm, past, present and into future generations in Yeshua's name, blood, and with a heavenly gold covering.

Adapted from Holly Schroeder Ubel.

CHAPTER TEN

Court of Heaven Session

If you have never done a Court of Heaven session, there are many books and YouTube videos available to give a much more in-depth explanation. For the sake of simplicity, this will be a brief outline you can follow.

You have the right and freedom to take it as far as you feel you should, and like the previous one, can come back as often as needed. It is all done by faith, and Holy Spirit will guide you as needed. The following is a portion of the quick guide that I have put together.

Court of Heaven Prayer Protocol Quick Guide

This guideline is to assist you in the Courts of Heaven. You can expand upon it as things come up. Allow and trust Holy Spirit to guide you. I purposely have done each one a bit differently to give an example as it's easy to get stuck on one methodology. I have found that it's not so much about the words and getting everything perfect as it is about our intention.

Always enter the Courtroom as you would any here, honoring and acknowledging Father as Judge, Yeshua as your Advocate, and Holy Spirit as your Counselor.

* Ask for full disclosure of accusations and divorce papers from the specific thing(s) for why you are in Court. In this case, we are asking for litigation and legislation against the Enemy by bringing evidence of him breaking the laws of love, bringing pain, loss, trauma, etc., throughout our life and bloodline. Be as specific as you can. You can ask for the vial of tears to be brought in as evidence.
* Confess the specific things revealed.
* Ask for forgiveness on behalf of self and bloodline all the way backward and forwards. Go as deep and thorough as possible.
* Forgive those who have harmed you and/or your bloodline, and ask Father to do the same. Where parents and leaders are concerned, it is important to include dishonor as it carries a heavy penalty. Holding judgment, offense, and/or unforgiveness against parents, even if they are in the wrong, has very negative consequences for us. Therefore, it is good to include confessing the sin of dishonor while forgiving them.

LIES: especially attached to trauma, name them specifically. Example: FATHER, I confess that when _____ happened, I believed the lie that_____. I change my mind (repent) of believing that lie and all of the damage it has done in my heart and my relationship with You and others. I ask for Your forgiveness, cleansing, and healing.

Now from my spirit seated in Messiah, by the authority He has given me, with all of my being I come out of the agreement and refuse that lie. I pull it out of my being and nail to the Cross every agreement, contract, covenant, vow, oath, all hidden documents, evil verdicts, bitter root judgment or expectation, curse or promise, and all documentation connected with it; along with all familiar spirits, their underlings, and all entities involved with this lie. I ask that You take a net of fire and gather up everything connected with it and remove it from my being. By doing so, I remove their rights to me and apply Yeshua's blood to erase the accusations against me.

Through Yeshua's power and blood, I erase the effects of that lie out of every part of my conscious, sub-conscious, and unconscious being-all of my DNA. Lord, I invite You to come and write the Truth in every place where that lie was and breathe Your breath of life into those areas and reign there from now on. Thank You, Father, for all that You have done in my heart. I receive Your forgiveness, cleansing, and healing into every part of my being.

VOWS: Be as specific as possible, ask Holy Spirit to help you. Bitterroot judgments include statements like, "I will never," "they are always," type statements. FATHER, I confess that when_____ happened, that I made a vow to _____. I change my mind about that vow and ask for your forgiveness, cleansing, and healing from its effects.

From my spirit seated in Messiah and by His power and authority, on behalf of my entire being I now revoke that vow and pull it out, nailing it to the Cross along with every agreement, covenant, contract, oath, promise, curse, bitter root judgment or expectation, all hidden documents, evil verdicts and all entities including familiar spirits and their underlings connected with it. I apply Yeshua's blood to erase it completely. I cancel all enemy rights that came with that trauma and vow, and receive Your forgiveness, cleansing, and healing from the effects of that it in every area of my being—conscious, sub-conscious, and unconscious being—soul, body, and head.

I ask that You teach me how to count on You and others in a healthy way, and correct everything that vow did in my heart and my relationships. I give You my will, Father, in every place where that vow was. Yeshua, I invite You to reign in my relational heart from this day forward. Thank You, Father, for delivering me.

* With other bloodline and personal issues that come up that you confess as sin, nail to Yeshua's cross every agreement, covenant, contract, oath, vow, **bitter root judgment and expectation, curse, promise, familiar spirit and their underlings, and every entity connected.

* Apply Yeshua's blood and living waters to erase all of the handwriting of ordinances against you, and on every altar in every dimension where your name(s) have been traded upon, and ask for angels to be released to eradicate those altars completely.

* Receive Father's forgiveness, cleansing, and healing all the way down into your soul and DNA.

* Offer the specific trauma to Him from the bloodline issues as both sin and trauma cause soul wounds, and ask Him to come and take it out of your soul, body, and head— every place it has lodged in your being, along with every hook, device, tuning fork, implant, thorn, or magnet.

* Ask Him to replace it with what you want instead and apply it there. Example, if fear, you could ask for love since His perfect love casts out all fear; or for peace, etc.

* Engage whatever it is He is replacing and thank Him for it.

* Receive divorce papers by faith and place them in your belly. (Ezekiel was told to eat the scroll)

* Often at this point, the Lord or someone in the Court will give something, so wait and see/listen and not rush off. He is so generous and loves to give good gifts to His children to replace what we have given Him during this time. It is all done by faith.

* I like to end with communion. By doing so, I am applying the body and blood of Yeshua to my DNA erasing the record from what

I had just worked on, as well as to reactivate our covenant. I celebrate it, exchange His life for mine and mine for His, erasing the record of death which is in the sin and iniquity by applying His words from John 6 - that if I eat of His flesh and drink of His blood, I will not die but live forever, nor will I hunger or thirst again. It's a way of sealing what has just happened, as I trade on the body and blood of Yeshua for greater intimacy since that was the whole purpose of His death and resurrection. For God so loved the world that He gave His Son.

You may want to go through this often and as thoroughly as possible, especially in areas with familiar patterns that continue or when new things come to mind. It is a subtle thing that can be so familiar that it goes unnoticed.

I encourage you to check in with this while doing these protocols. You can offer thanksgiving, praise, and worship for all that has transpired. Bless and seal it, asking that the angels release the Divorce Papers and Verdicts on Earth as in Heaven, as well as putting copies into the archives.

*I have used the Sanford's teaching on Bitter Root Judgments and Expectations for years. With the Court of Heaven Protocol, I have found this understanding to be critical in getting to root issues. Whenever there is a pattern, I am often drawn to this and have found much freedom personally and in assisting others. So I have come up with a protocol from various teachings of others which include: The Praying Medic, Katie Souza, Splankna, Theophostic/Transformation Prayer, Ian Clayton, Robert Henderson, Kym Whitman, Dan Duval, and others.

CHAPTER ELEVEN

Happy Tears

I want to end this book celebrating what we have together discovered about tears. I desire that you will have a healthier relationship with tears. To treasure each one that you shed as you recognize each is stored in a vial of liquid pearl, along with their record that Father holds dearly

Isaiah 25:8 (EXB)

He will destroy [swallow up] death forever [1 Cor. 15:54].
The Lord God will wipe away every tear from every face
[Rev. 7:17; 21:4]. He will take away the shame [disgrace] of
his people from the earth. The Lord has spoken.

1 Corinthians 15:26, 54-55, 57 (EXB and TLV)

The last enemy to be destroyed is death. So when this body that can be destroyed [is perishable/corruptible] will clothe itself with that which can never be destroyed [is imperishable/incorruptible], and this body that dies [mortal] will clothe itself with that which can never die [immortality], then this Scripture will be made true [come to pass]: "Death is destroyed forever [swallowed up] in victory [Is. 25:8].
[L O] Death, where is your victory? Death, where is your pain [Hos. 13:14]?" But thanks be to God, who keeps giving us the victory through our Lord Yeshua the Messiah!

We are overcoming death as we free our bloodlines from the record of death. Yeshua said in John 14, that if we eat His flesh and drink His blood, we will not die but live forever. Taking these elements and applying the truth of His words erases the record of sin and death just like the woman I mentioned whose DNA markers have disappeared from taking communion daily in this way.

When He said, *"It is finished,"* He completed all that for us to discard mortality and put on immortality! The old man died, we are now new creations *IN HIM* (2 Corinthians 5:17)!

Let's not waste our pain, but embrace and celebrate that our tears, mourning, pain, and suffering are falling away. He is keeping each of our tears in a safe place and one day will wipe them away once and for all!

Revelation 21:4 regarding the New Jerusalem (TPT):

He will wipe away every tear from their eyes and eliminate death. No one will mourn or weep any longer. The pain of wounds will no longer exist, for the old order has ceased.

So let's end this book with happy tears!

Tears of hope.

Tears of laughter.

Tears of stress relief.

Tears of anticipation.

Tears of joy at long-awaited news

A long-held desire fulfilled.

Death destroyed.

Tree of Life.

Restored.

Now go out and laugh until you cry, and let joy be your warfare!

◆◆◆

ABOUT THE AUTHOR

 Pam Holecheck has been in ministry for 30 years and traveled to 45 nations teaching and training. She has worked with YWAM (Youth With A Mission) on staff and leading schools, as well as working with churches, Houses of Prayer, and other ministries. After living in Germany for 11 years, she moved back to America due to her Mother's terminal illness. This is her first book where you will get an authentic glimpse into the often overlooked side to ministry life. Pam is available to speak, teach, or minister and can be reached at pholecheck@googlemail.com.

FOOTNOTES:

1. Hans Jenny http://old.world-mysteries.com/sci_cymatics.htm

2. The KJV translates Strongs H6743; something prolonged or tall, i.e., a vial. H4997: bottle as in wine.

3. Topography of Tears. See photos and full article at http://www.rose-lynnfisher.com/tears.html

4. Joseph Stromberg http://www.smithsonianmag.com/science-nature/the-microscopic-structures-of-dried-human-tears-180947766/?no-ist

5. Dr. Masaru Emoto, "The Hidden Messages in Water" ISBN 978074328980

6. Sid Roth, "It's Supernatural" Dennis Walker at about the14 minutes mark.

7. Strong's Concordance, From ס.פ.ר (H5608)

8. Doug Addison: https://dougaddison.com/2018/05/a-vision-from-heaven-new-promotions-and-alliances-forming-episode-52/

9. http://www.roberthenderson.org/ and https://prayingmedic.com/

10. Joey Letourneau Elijah List http://www.elijahlist.com/words/display_word.html?ID=13768

11. https://www.webmd.com/balance/features/why-we-cry-the-truth-about-tearing-up#1

Made in the USA
Columbia, SC
29 March 2019